ISBN-13: 9798987474204 (Paperback)
ISBN-13: 9798987474211 (eBook)
ISBN-13: 9798987474228 (Hardcover)

Printed in the United States of America

# Contents

# Content Guidance & Images

This book explores aspects of mental health challenges and contains depictions of self-harm, physical and sexual abuse. These aspects may be difficult for some readers. **Please read with care.**

## Images

All images used in this book are royalty-free, available for public download and use and were obtained legally for that purpose.

# The Shaping of a Diamond

## a Diamond

By Desiree Batiste

I dedicate this book to all the people and influences that have shaped the experiences which have made me who I am today. First and foremost, I want to thank God for the strength that sustained me during all those dark times, his love which helped me to keep my faith and the gift of the written word which he has so graciously bestowed upon me. I am so humbled that you gave me another chance at life, when even people in my own family would not do the same. You gave me a glimpse of who I could become if I had the courage and drive to achieve it, and you never left my side...even during the darkest of hours. I am forever thankful for all the many blessings you bestowed upon me, for your love and guidance and for your forgiveness.

To my wonderful husband, Michael: You and I spent so many years apart...as halves missing our better part. I always felt like I was only a fraction of what I could be if I just had more courage, more love, more self-esteem. I know that most people say that you cannot get those things from outside yourself - it has to come from within, but my 'within' happened to be such a bottomless cavern of longing and self-hatred that it was never going to heal without you... my soulmate, my one true love. You are the only one that has ever been able to look at and truly see the real ME. You and I have really been through hell...both before we met, and even after...with the stressful situations we found ourselves up against. You had to help me to get all of the toxic leaches out of my life one by one, and most of them did not want to respect our wishes and just let us live our lives. They tried to ruin our happiness and poison our family before we even had a chance to really become a family. You spent so much time pouring love into our family and strength into me trying to heal my heart from all its past damage that you did not leave a reserve behind for yourself. That is your way... you give 150%, unselfishly and with no expectations in return.

When that kicked off our nightmare journey that started early September and which has finally wrapped up recently, I worried if our love would be strong enough to get us through it all, but again, God knew better than I did, and we are stronger and even more in love than ever. Though there are some very RAW emotions in some of the poems that I wrote during that rough time, I just want you to remember that I do not hold it against you or blame you in any way, nor will I tolerate anyone else trying to do so. You were far stronger than you should have had to be for far too long, and that is always a recipe for cracks in the walls and foundation. I am just glad that we are repairing and rebuilding together. I will love you with every part of me until time unending. You are the one who gave reason to my rhyme, and I will ALWAYS be thankful for God seeing fit to bring us together at last.

To my charming daughter, Kaylee: We also have seen our relationship have its ups and downs and there was a time that I worried that you were starting to hate me. I know with how rough life was for us that I likely had that coming. God knows I did not make very smart decisions in the past, and a lot of the ones I made caused us both tremendous heartaches. I feel very blessed to be your mother, and very lucky to have you as my daughter. You are funny, outspoken, talented, determined and beautiful inside and out. You will go on to do great things in life and I will be just as proud of you then as I am now. Just know that I owe you big time for all those times which I leaned on you when it was not your job to hold me up and deal with my problems when you had so many of your own. Sometimes angels don't have wings, they have crop tops and platform shoes and I know you are my angel and I love you more than you'll ever know. I hope that this book inspires you to dream big, knowing that dreams don't always have to stay dreams forever. It was a long journey to get here, and I am glad I got to share a lot of the duration of it with you.

To my son, Aaron: Our relationship has always been a loving one, but as you know...in my long laundry list of regrets, your childhood and how that all unfolded is high on that list. I know we can only go forward now because the past cannot be re-written, but just know that in a perfect world...you and your sister would not have had to grow up in a broken home and away from each other. We would have all been a family...one mom, one dad and zero yelling. I am so proud of the man you have grown into and of not only what you have already achieved but of the goals that you have for yourself. You know more about who you are at your age then I did at that same age. Heck, I am still in the process of healing and figuring out who I am - REALLY am. But I want to thank you for all of the encouragement which you have given me during this journey, the advice, but most importantly, the love. You and Kaylee will always be two of the three creations that I made in this life for which I have no regrets, with the last creation being this book.

To my friends: You have all stood by me, listened to me whine and bitch and cry and moan and lament my life and my misfortunes. You never wavered in your belief in my strength or my passion for what I wanted to do with my life. You knew that my stubborn determination would not let me give up on this dream, and so it makes me especially proud to be able to place a copy of this book in your hands...so you can take this journey with me, into the wilder, darker, scarier stops in my past. Once you have a better understanding of what you helped hold me together through, I think you will be even more amazed at my stubborn tenacity. I love you guys, and here's to decades more friendship in the future with way less tears.

To my three cats: Sketch, Pixel and Trace. Someone will read this dedication to you. Thank you for all of those snuggles on the couch or in my bed. When I was down and at my most alone, your little hearts could feel it and reached out to give me comfort. I will never forget that, and I will always be here to give you comfort and love when you need me.

To anyone who bought this book: Thank you for taking this journey. I promise, it will be a very interesting one. Thank you in advance for giving attention to these poor words of mine and just know that no matter how alone any of us may feel at any point in our lives, the one thing that we all have in common with one another is the experience of tragedy. I hope that my tear-choked path, which ultimately lead me to happiness leads you to somewhere that, at the bare minimum, gives you more solid ground under you while you figure out the rest of your journey. We are all in this together!

My love to each and every one of you. -Desiree

# Introduction

The experiences of my life served to do one very important thing. No matter how hard I was hit or how much pressure I was under, these moments helped the "me" who stands here now to take shape. The hits made me unbreakable, the cuts gave me facets of depth, the pressure helped to bring out my many sides and my shine. The poems I have included in this book cover some memorable moments in my life going from childhood through present day. I didn't pull any punches or sugar coat anything. If there was a moment I hated, you'll know it. If there was a moment I treasured, you'll feel it. If there were times I almost gave up, you'll know why. If there were people who deliberately made my life more painful and difficult, you will get to meet them in my poems.

There are also poems which cover those going through their own rough journey and crossing paths with mine at that time. Sometimes the experience created in these moments was like throwing kerosene on a grease fire...highly volatile and unpleasant. That doesn't mean that is the way the situation stayed forever. Each moment in our lives (either good or bad) is only ours for the briefest of moments, until it is replaced with another moment, and another, and another. Some experiences led to better, happier times. Others led to darker times. Others led to endings...some fated, some ill-fated, some bittersweet, some necessary. All things will end at some point in time. The idea is to be happy with where you ended up when the story finally draws to a close. My journey is still in progress, but I have to say I think I am at least finally on the path to a bright future and am ever blessed to have those by my side who are a part of the story.

# Facet 1: Childhood

The poems in this section were written about experiences in my childhood. I grew up in what started out to be a loving household. My father was a Vietnam veteran who was disabled after the war and heavily medicated for a whole host of health problems and a few misdiagnosed ones. He was not allowed to care for me or to speak up against my abusive, unhinged mother. Until I became a teenager, my mother and I were extremely close. I looked up to her. She spoiled me with gifts, toys, clothes, movies, meals out. All the kids in the neighborhood wished their moms were as great as mine. She was often the only person I thought was a true friend to me, and I wanted to grow up to be just like her. That all changed when I became a teenager. As soon as I showed signs of wanting to have a life outside of her vision of what my life should end up being or do things on my own, I became the enemy, and she became something worse than any Disney movie villain. I could never imagine just how far she would go to get what she wanted or what she was truly capable of.

Before the main tragedy came a mini one. The loss of my innocence, which quickly led to additional painfully bad decisions such as smoking, and attempted suicide. These moments are captured in my poems, "The Light" and "Puppets" while my suicidal thoughts and moment are captured in the poems "Sleep" and "Nothing Is Real".

# The Light

I was only eight
I remember like it was yesterday
The heavy, oppressive weight
The night he took the light away

I had been full of innocence
Dreams and love in my eyes
In the darkness, full of suspense
Just how dark, I was soon to realize

He said we were playing a game
My head then hit a table
Nothing was ever again the same
My world became unstable

I woke not knowing what happened
I just knew something was wrong
My happiness forever dampened
I tried so hard to be strong

My head had a bump on the back
My panties were across the room
My light had faded to black
His evil presence did loom

I felt pain
I felt shame
I felt rage
I felt blame

I tried to cope with what he had done
I tried to let it go
After all, he was the pastor's son
And he thought no one would ever know

I masked the pain by smoking
I tried to fake a smile
But the sadness left me choking
Just a mess, no longer a child

I tried to tell my mother years later
She finally believed but would not aid
Instead of shoulder to cry on, she was a traitor
I told his parents, but they said to stop the charade

I walled my heart off to life
I swore to never trust
Raw pain that cut like a knife
Because of another's lust

I spent five years in mourning
Pushing everyone away
Until I met the first boy I loved
Who came to save the day

We were fourteen
He loved me completely
Never cross or mean
Held on to me so sweetly

I held on to love two years
Until one fateful day
One of my greatest fears
Came true and he was taken away

Car crash, a drunk at the wheel
His ribcage crushed in, so much pain
They said he was gone, I dropped to kneel
I knew without him I'd go insane

A later mistake would bring back my light
But that's another tale
One that holds a chance I might
Overcome this darkness and prevail

# *Puppets*

We slept in the same bed up until the end
You always said it was because I was insecure
The truth was that I was your only friend
You had become a hermit, so obscure

I spent years as your Barbie doll
Sitting perfect on the shelf
Before I even knew how to crawl
All because you hated yourself

You saw my life as your second chance
To take credit for successes you failed to achieve
Though I cried, you never took a second glance
You had convinced yourself what to believe

In your eyes, I was content
Because you gave me everything you thought mattered
Instead, my days were spent
Trying to hold together what you shattered

You called me a whore
Made sure I knew I was going to hell
The biggest burdensome chore
Was trying to make you well

Your mind told you that you had every illness
For years, I pushed you around in a wheelchair
You piled upon me more and more stress
You did it just to keep me prisoner there

You withdrew me from school with a lie
Locked away over two years with you
Determined I was going to live your way or die
The more I tried to fight, the more you would do

Locked in a trunk that you would beat on the outside
I learned to fear loud noises and thunder
You demonized all I was that you couldn't abide
You stole my innocent child-like wonder

You handcuffed me when you'd beat me
You kicked me until I couldn't breathe
You threatened to discard me
You said I was someone you would no longer need

You raised me to think dreaming of my soulmate was sin
The penalty for disobeying you would be death
You sat there with your mocking, evil grin
Each time you called me 'Beth'

I learned to deal with what you did to me
But what truly broke my heart
Is what I slowly started to see
You doing to tear my father apart

You took over his money
You decided when he could have things
I know you thought it was so funny
Watching the once proud eagle with clipped wings

It took less time to beat him down
Than it ever did with me
While I was your puppet, he was your clown
But his love for you would not let him see

Fear let him sit silent while you planned to end me
Fear froze him when your plan took shape
Although he prayed for both of us on bended knee
We both knew there was no escape

I got lucky though – foster care rescued me
Got a chance to live the life I was denied
I knew someday the world would finally see
The "me" that had been trapped so long inside

The guilt locked away in my soul
For leaving him behind with her
Eventually would take its toll
As the details passed in a blur

It took years of talking to others to figure it out
What she had done to him that night
All my regrets became one tortured shout
Knowing I could never make it right

She used his health against him
She never took no for an answer
She took his life away from him
She was his worst cancer

She waited in the darkness
She waited, sight unseen
Her intent to lay him to rest
As she turned off his C-Pap machine

He saw the monster behind the blond, blue eyed mask
He refused to break or bow
When she decided to ask
If he would renew his vow

She gained sympathy from others for her grief
Theatrics real for dishonest means
Her callousness beyond belief
As she continued her schemes

It took years of asking questions to uncover the lie
And learn of your true fate
Now I am left asking why
He figured out what she is too late

Survivors guilt is real
I wish I could have saved my dad
Though they say time will heal
He was all that I ever had


We shared the common misery
Of having our freedom wrenched away
And I know in heaven that he sees
That I miss him every day

We're both safe from her in our own way
Though life can never be the same
The only revenge I get is the satisfaction to not say
Think or ever speak of her name

# Sleep

From the time of my birth
All I've wanted is rest
Since being on this earth
I've always tried my best

But life sat there
Like an immovable, impassible cloud
And pounded in its stare
My happiness it did enshroud

"God", I said, "Close my eyes, please
Let me go to sleep
Living hasn't brought me what I need
All I do is weep"
But still I stayed
He wouldn't let me check out
There was only one way:
To ask someone to show me what sleep was about

One day, as luck would have it
My travels had taken me far
And in my last moving moment
Was placed in the path of a car

Hurled and pushed
Tossed, in fact
Completely squashed
And dropped on my back

Rushed to the emergency room

And God now looks the other way
My life has sealed my doom
I go to sleep today

I heard the doctor say to mom
"There's nothing we can do"
As I lay in a peaceful calm
And begun to turn grey blue

Then – One last breath
One last flinch
I am introduced to death
Quick as a pinch

They close my eyes back home
As they start to weep
I guess it's 'cause they realized
That I had gone to sleep

# Nothing Is Real

She walked down the powdered hallway to the shadowed door

Hit the candy-coated steps leading west

Wanting reality less and fantasy more

Because life had lost its zest

Her feet hit the plastic concrete

Her mind wanders through a timeless place

Where the killers heal and the honest men cheat

The clock in the hall stands with no face


All is nothing, the echo repeats - Nothing is real


Turning the crooked corner to a path leading nowhere

But intending to follow as far is it takes her

People who have to listen can't- the rest just don't care

And still aren't prepared for what occurs

Lying in the darkness of a silk coated room

Lost in thoughts that bury you alive

What could be love is clearly not, the brightness turned to gloom

And the only question repeats again – Why? Why? Why?


All is nothing, the echo repeats- Nothing is Real


Hearing the shatter of a noiseless, transparent glass

Turning to face your doom and welcome it in

Trying to get by, trying to get through – you can't pass

You have just been captured by your sin

You close your eyes to see the light

You pray its pain won't hurt you
Even though you know it might
You pray the hurt won't touch you
Silently, it creeps in and snuffs out the candle of life
Motionless, you lay there accepting- you can face no more strife

All is nothing, the echo repeats- Nothing is real.... not even the pain you feel

# The Promise

The three hundred pills went down
with a thud
Sitting in the alcohol cocktail I threw
on top of them
My eyes grew heavy, I felt like crud
A tragic end to a tragic femme

My body and soul began to separate
I threw up but I couldn't feel it
I knew by then it was way too late
A broken heart with no way to heal it

My eyes opened somewhere else
I was floating above the ground on my back
Was this some kind of evil spell?
It felt like I was under attack

The landscape around me was brown and dead
I've never felt such fear
My mind just wanted to be back in my bed
Or anywhere else but here

I felt a dread heavier than a ton of bricks
It started to choke my soul
Suicide was clearly one of the devil's tricks
And falling for it, I had lost control

I remember a tear coming out of my eye
Me realizing it was too late
The worry in me grew and I couldn't say why

Likely because I started grasping my fate

I thought to myself, 'I wish I could start over'
But I knew I had no chance
In hell, there are no four-leaf clover
So, I just zoned out into a trance

Then I felt a shift of direction
A pull of the flow
Before I could have a minute of reflection
A change of speed, and off I go

It was no longer a death desert
That was gone in a blink
The landscape began to convert
Before I could even think

When I focused my vision, I just saw light
And I peered into its center
I felt love, strength and might
Because I sat before my mentor

I knew him immediately, his eyes were piercing
Like tiffany-stained glass windows
He was surrounded by a beautiful green meadow clearing
Over top of my amazement, his voice rose

"Why can't you see your beauty
As I see it in my heart?
You've gone from being just moody
To tearing yourself apart"

I could see how I looked in the reflection of his eyes
I was not ugly and small
It was then it sunk in, and I realized
The enormity of it all

This was God…there was no more doubt
He cared for me more than anyone ever had
In my stupidest time of need, he helped me out
Helped to bring something good out of something bad

He told me that he was proud of me
And that I would get my second chance
There was one condition, you see
As I looked around at the great expanse

He said, "Make me a promise now
That you will never throw your life away
I need to hear you vow
That you know why you need to stay"

I was honest and said it hurt too much losing love
Having Mark ripped away
I said it's easy to ask things like that when he's above
And doesn't have to feel this way

He told me that I was mistaken
He had lost loved ones too
Even though I felt forsaken
He was there to see me through

He didn't want me to be among the lost
He said that I'd always have love
But to never pay so high a cost
Thinking to punch out early and return to him above

I still had life to live
I still had things to do
I still had much to give
I knew it all was true

My mind tried to process this
God is real, he is here
But back home were others who began to miss
Me because I wasn't near

I woke up in the hospital
Tears running down my face
I'm just a stupid teenager, not an apostle
Who the hell will believe this wild goose chase?!

Something told me it didn't matter
Whether anyone else believes
There would always be negative chatter
From Satan and all those he deceives

I'd just have to live my life well
Let my outcome be my story
Since he saved me from the depths of hell
To give me one more shot, for his glory

# Facet 2: High School

My high school career started off two years delayed due to the abuse I had suffered at the hands of my mother. The foster care system had me tested to determine where to place me in school and I started out as a junior in high school. Due to being behind, I was going to have to do two senior years in order to have enough credits to graduate. This was all a bit much being thrown at me. For the first time in the three years of hell that I endured at my mother's hands, I was free. I didn't know for how long, since despite logic of how sick people can be, the foster care system's goal is to "reunite families, not separate kids from parents" but sometimes, that is exactly what needs to happen. During this time when it was up in the air as to whether or not I would be sent back home or not, I decided to lose my virginity, get high, get drunk and do every stupid, reckless thing you could possibly think of. I knew if I was sent home, I would end up buried in the backyard of my childhood home...so I figured if I was going to have a life cut short, then I might as well have some experiences that would justify a kid getting killed by their parent. In retrospect, this was a STUPID outlook to have. For the first time in my life, I was in control of my life, and instead of savoring that opportunity and being real with myself to figure out what I WANTED out of life, I instead did every dumb thing imaginable so that I could flip my mother the invisible 'fuck you' middle finger and have the last laugh. But I was the one who had to deal with how all of that made me feel. I was already coming off of how I felt after my first love, Mark, had been killed by a drunk driver. Now, I was also having to process that there really WAS/IS a GOD and an afterlife...and sit there and recount all of the dumb things I had done and worry if I had any chance of making it to heaven at that point. That is a lot

of stress for a sixteen-and-a-half-year-old teenager.

"What is Reality Inside of Me?" and "Our Worth" both cover the many ups and downs and revelations I began to have about God and what I needed in my life following my attempted suicide. It reflects exactly how I felt about everything in my life at that moment in time and helped to shed some light on that darkness. As I got older, approaching adulthood, my faith and understanding of the hereafter grew, and I share this in "God's Love – the Great Plan" and "What is Your Will?"

"Seduction" was written a few months after I foolishly threw my virginity away...and then went into my 'drunk-or-high-all-the-time' destructive phase and realized that everything I was doing to myself was further destroying me as I continued to try to find love by giving pieces of my soul away to those who did not deserve me. I wrote that one as if seduction was a living entity introducing itself and being honest about what it really is and what it does to people. It's like every one-night-stand loser who lied to me giving an introduction of themselves. In the poem "Hate", I follow much the same pattern of personification, making hate describe itself. Hate was definitely a feeling I knew very well in high school. People all mostly hated me and bullied me, and because I never did anything about it but turn my sadness inward, I really hated myself. It was this overwhelming hatred that almost drove me to suicide again. Thankfully...I ended up finding out I was pregnant with my son, so I bolted from school like a prisoner trying to escape confinement and got my G.E.D. diploma instead of subjecting myself to more torment from people who probably hated themselves even more than I hated myself at the time. Lastly in this section, "Things That Go Wrong" was my teenage observation of the day-to-day struggles facing many of us.

# What is Reality Inside of Me?

Living – a roller coaster ride

Pain – something we try to keep inside

Happiness – hard to get, hard to keep

People – a source of joy, the reason I weep

Love – walks in and out of your space

Alone – without, desolate. No one and no place

Crying – a natural reaction

My boyfriend – a pleasant distraction

Waking up – don't enjoy it anymore

My room – I rarely pass its door

Imprisoned – trapped, contained

Success – driving me insane

My face – the thing I'll go through life and never see

God – the person I would most like to be

Heaven – non-existent

People's hatred – too persistent

Anger – the essence of my personality

Failure – my destined reality

Wishes – that used to come true

Dreams – I got from you

Hopes – were lost

My soul – the cost

My goodness – mistreated

Lies – I didn't need that

Burning out – needing to rest

Feelings – put to the test

Winding down – losing drive

Pain increases – can't survive

Myself – the only one I serve

Fear enters – losing the nerve

Giving up – all I can do

Inferno of hell – what I've been put through

Down for the count – one last chance

Eyes half open – one last glance

Chest falling – one last breath

Invading peace – to face my death

Permanent – can't change my mind

Friends – the ones I leave behind

Acceptance – not a concern

Sanctitude – something to learn

My soul – free

No mourners – just me

Living – undone

Erased from memory – soon to come

Memories – all were fake

Sorrow – all I could take

Plan – shut my eyes tight

Progress – I see the light

Path taken – the one they barricaded

Screaming obscenities – was the way they serenaded

Ignore – the voices preventing me

Follow – the being of light I see

Pulled back – trapped by hate

Escape – embraced by fate

Knowledge – what I never knew

Beauty – what is real, what is true

Care – what he shows inside

Brick wall – crumbles to reveal the depth I hide

The best – what I could never be while living

Trying – all the words, the giving

Silence – more communication to us all

Uncaptivated – unshackled, my soul climbs tall

Ascent – to my cloud

Prayer – thought out loud

Confusion – at an end

The savior – my best friend

# Our Worth

How much am I worth?
Haven't we all asked that aloud?
It's a question since birth
Something none of us know much
about

People can tell us we are loved
But on whose scale do we weigh it?
They can tell us we're enough
But if they don't even know themselves, how can they say it?

I have heard people many a time
Say they'd give everything they had for someone
Just out of the blue – no reason or rhyme
It came rolling off their tongue

Then there's the people who give in to the pain
They throw away the gift of life before even opening it
As tears fall from their loved one's eyes like rain
They look heavenward, deep in regret

Did they do all they could
Say all they wanted to
Done all they should
To tell you they loved you?

Or did you decide your life
Was only worth the bullet you gave
Did you escape your bitter strife
Or take it to the grave?

I think our worth is above all material things
Houses, cars, and diamond rings

It's not your face, it's not your bod
It's the worth placed upon us from our father, God

You can make it what you choose
Just remember life's something to give, not lose

It can be as great as you make it
And no one can ruin it if you don't let them take it

It's the one thing you're in charge of – and we all know why
God let you have it 'til the day you die

# God's Love — The Great Plan

One week's work beyond compare
God's creation of the earth
And the gift of life, most rare
The dawn of beauty's birth

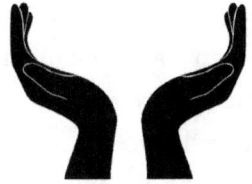

A gift to those who love him
A chance for those who might
But for those who don't, there's dark and dim
They had a chance to set things right

And when mistakes were made
God still paved us a way
He sent his son as the price to pay
And lo, he saved the day

Who has done as much as this to earn
All of our love?
Only God, our lord and savior
In heaven, up above

# What is Your Will?

A man wandered in off the street
And entered a solemn church
Intending to rest his feet
While he gave his soul a search

He knelt before the alter
And bent his knees to pray
Saying "I don't want to falter
Please show me the way

Lord, what is your will?
What do you want from me?
To make good out of ill?
To understand things I don't see?"

And the lord answered, "Many things do I desire
I want your love and respect
To keep you out of hell fire
It's your wrong I will detect

Let me in your heart
And I will heal your pain
When you're torn apart
My love washes over you like rain

I want your happiness in life
I want you to do your best
A chance to live a life free of strife
But don't forget the rest

To love your neighbor, life do savor
Give freely to everyone
Accepting the Father, Spirit, and Son

But most important, I desire your return
Home heavenward to my ever-loving arms
I don't want any of my children to burn
I want them safe from harm

So go and proclaim to others
What I have told you now
To all your sisters and brothers
And I will show you how"

So, the man stood and left
Walked out to the street
No longer quite so bereft
Able to stand tall on his feet

He went around to everyone
Preaching the will of the savior
About the Father, Spirit, and Son
His words boosted lives with flavor

He can't reach everyone everywhere
No matter how far he'd roam
So here lies the words he wishes to share
Contained within this poem

# Seduction

I think I'll begin with a brief introduction
On the torrid art form of seduction
If you've never been through it, pay attention
To all the things nobody bothered to mention
I start off sly and earn your trust
Use the word 'love', but behind it is all lust
I take your goodness; I mess up your mind
I'll help you make me so important; you'll leave everything behind
I'll take your heart and tear it all apart
Mess with your soul until you freely give in
I'll change you for the worse and hide it from your face
I'll disappear awhile until it's me you start to chase
I'll lie right to your face, and you'll let me do it
Anything and everything I can do, I'll put you through it
I'll get everything I can from you and then be gone
Pack up, leave town and quickly move on
I'll move so fast; you won't know what hit you
You were dumb enough to think that I'd stick with you
I'll find someone else who's naïve like you
Someone else I can do this to
I'll keep going 'til I get caught or die
'Cause we're talking seduction – the art of the lie

# Hate

I'm the disease of hate
The child of lust and sadness
I can make your life great
And fill your soul with madness
I instill in you a desire
To hurt and mistreat the rest
And then backed by a hell bound fire
To put the pain on yourself next
I am very contagious
And can be passed with just a glare
I make you act outrageous
As you pass me everywhere
The only way to get rid of me
Is to choose to not let me in
I try to hide it so that you won't see
I am the root of all sin
I am the source of every problem
I am the cause of every wrong
I infect child, woman, and man
And make it impossible to get along
I can be passed on for no reason
And infect someone who never had me
No matter what the year or time or season
I can cause your heart to stop and bleed
Even if you say you won't let me in your heart
I'll find a way to get inside
And once I do, I'll tear you all apart
You'll be in for a hell of a ride

# Things That Go Wrong

People crazy, running around
Life is twist-turned upside down
Prayers said aloud to ears that don't listen
Having six toilets but there is no kitchen
Doing your best, and losing in the end
Gaining two enemies and losing a friend
Your poor next-door neighbor is a rich snob
And the street corner bum beat you in for a job
Looks like you're down and out on your luck
Way out of whack, life is starting to suck
The flowers bought yesterday are dead tonight
Too many wrongs to stop and make right
The blind guy hears what the deaf one can't
The deaf one sees what the blind one shan't
You look out the window at the end of your day
Just in time to see them tow your car away
You can't go home 'cause the keys are in the trunk
You're starting to think, "What is all this bunk?
What the hell's goin' on here lately?
Maybe God has it in for me"
So much confusion in a peaceful world
Where girl meets boy but is stolen by girl
But that right there is not the worst of your trouble
Hey honey, hate to burst your bubble
But the guy who left you a month ago
Who said, "come on, let's do it, I'll go slow"
He's disappeared, no goodbye or maybe
And left you here to have his baby

The water bill is overdue
They say, "pay or we will sue"
They shut off the phone, now you can't get calls
Boy, they sure have a lot of balls
The electric people say, "hurry up
We've given you time, two months is enough"
Your house is foreclosed, and you're on your way out
This is what freedom is all about?
Drama enough to make you hurl
Too bad, so sad – welcome to the real world

# Facet 3: Learning to Adult

One of the hardest things that anyone can go through is losing someone. But, when that someone was such a key part of your life, losing them seems like something you may not ever be able to move past. After the sting of losing Mark subsided, I began to use the pain of loss to try to see if I could figure out how to 'adult' once I hit age 18 and make a life for myself that he would be proud of and happy to see me live. "Love's Bond Eternal" is all about my journey to hoping that I didn't break my promise to God again and that I would live a life worth living until one day, I got to see Mark again.

Of course, things don't always turn out the way that you plan them to, but I did not give up. I tried hard to try to build up some self esteem and belief in myself and see if that would lead me to better things and stronger ground. I talk about the regret that I had for the failed relationship between me and my son's father in "Season's Passed". Following that, "If" and "Life is" are times when I took a good hard look at myself and was real with what I saw and tried to get through to myself that I did not have to see myself the way that others (especially unsupportive, toxic family members) saw me.

However, adult life turned out to be every bit as hard and scary as I thought it was going to be. I had hoped that when I became an adult, that the scary moments and the pain I had already survived would be distant memories and that better things were in store for me. However, sometimes in life it seems like the only constant we have is disappointment, and that is sure how I felt! "Lost Love" covers the complicated situation of being in a relationship with one person while being unable to let go of a relationship that did not work out, but that you still feel obligated to fight to revive. I know we have all been there at least once! Finally, "Ramblings of a Stranger" is a dark wandering through my mind at a particular time of chaos...reflecting on how I felt after my suicide and realizing that I was not yet who I really wanted to be.

# Love's Bond Eternal

If I could hold time in my hands
Like I've held you in my arms
Would I save the fragile sands
And keep them safe from harm?

If a smile could tell you every thought
That I could ever hold
Would I ignore all I had been taught
So that my story may be told?

If I was guaranteed forever
To do with what I please
Would I be thankful and remember
Or spend eternity on my knees?

If one minute of redemption
Could end a lifetime of pain
Would I resist temptation
Or be set up to fall again?

If tomorrow never came
Would I say I'd done enough
Content I never achieved fame
Appreciative that life was rough?

These are questions I must ask
Now that we have parted ways
This has made in me the task
To cherish the rest of my days

It seems that we are worlds apart
And it's hard to not feel alone
Gone from my side, now you're next to God's heart
You were an earth angel on loan

You've made in me the need to try
And see that my ways get mended
My tear-streaked face pointed to the sky
Until I reach the gates of heaven

One day I'll be before the gates of pearl
And watch as they open wide
You will be my guide in that next new world
After God shows me inside

There will be no more sorrow
Gone will be all the pain
And an endless supply of tomorrows
As we help God pour out the rain

# Season's Passed

As the leaves fall from the trees

And another year has gone

I get up from my knees

And wonder 'Where did I go wrong?'

Those here today are gone by spring

Choosing to forget our history

Perhaps it's a painful remembering

Or trying to solve the mystery

Why is it the more things change

The more they seem the same

The more I think I find it strange

The only thing different about each man was their name

Despite the tears you cry

Forgetting the passage of time

Masking the pain inside

Ignoring that reason has no rhyme

You take on what you can

To protect the smile of your child

Without letting them know this man

Wasn't a dad, but a hormone run wild

All you can say is the season's passed away

And like a river's course it always seems to change

You may not have tomorrow what you have today

Leaving you only with memories as you age

# If

If all you see is anger
Then you need to look at my life
To understand the feelings of a stranger
Try to sympathize with their strife

If all you see is ugliness
Then I think you are shallow, truly
When you should be seeing the tenderness
That comes from an inner beauty

If all you see is the bad in me
Then you should try facing the mirror
Because there's bad in everyone, you see
And understanding draws people nearer

If all you see is a person who
Needs to be loved and cherished
Then I guess this poem finally got through
Before this person perished

I guess now it's pretty clear
And very plain to see
That I'm just a person with love, hope and fear
And that's all I'll ever be

# Lost Love

The one I loved, I lost
The one who loves me stays
Who can calculate the cost
Of love that's lost both ways?

Is it wrong to be true to one
Even though your heart belongs to another?
When love shines brighter than the sun
Shouldn't you tell each other?

How do you know when it's love
Or whether it's just a dream?
Is there some sign from above
That this isn't what it seems?

Maybe I'm wrong for choosing
The one who won't notice I exist
Because it will always be me who is lost
When you are last on their list

But it's wrong not to follow your heart
Or say how you really feel
Even when it's tearing you apart
You should speak what you know is real

I will always love him
But he will still be gone
Even though the other choices seem dim
Trying again is not wrong

# Life Is

Life is sometimes hard
It can make you want to stop
Sadness can tear you apart
Until you feel you might drop

Life is sometimes confusing
Makes you wonder why you're here
As you sit in silence pursuing
Your hidden, inner fear

Life is also frightening
Like a storm in the night
It can change in a flash like lightning
And give you new insight

Life is precious
And should be lived completely
Without any regrets
And treasured in memories, sweetly

But mostly, life is a wonderment
Simple and free
Full of the treasures
Bestowed upon thee

As simple as lifting a flower
Out of a garden of pain
So that in a heavy shower
It doesn't have to drown in the rain

You carry it gently
So it won't wither and die
Bring it with you to see
This brand-new sky

No matter how dark today may seem
Or how cold it may feel
Never could life be too extreme
Simply because it's real

Always remember that life is a gift
Wrapped in fate, and opened with love
Use it to always uplift
You to achieve all you dream of

# Ramblings of a Stranger

Is the love I miss
Greater than the love left behind?
When I search for the answer
Is it only a question I'll find?

Looking for assurance
In a closet of doubt
Seeking the insurance
To get to never do without

Needing what I can't get
Having what I don't want
Memories made to forget
In a clouded nonchalance

The security I saw disappeared
The loneliness echoed to my heart
Pounding in my darkest fear
Tearing the delusion apart

What I thought perfect was flawed
What I saw as love was hate
Just as fast as defrosted thaw
My emotions stirred at hell's gate

A place I knew, a place I'd been
Strange, and wrong, and leery
But with a greater peace than I'd ever seen
That calmed my aching weary

Will the familiar produce the latter
To my heart's full bliss?
Or will my ever-aching life
Be cursed by the devil's kiss?

The one who sees, looks not
The one who hears, speaks not
'Tis a forbidden testimony
To an ever-faithful plot

The life's legacy, its reap
Its fulfillment is its end
Will your life end in a heap
With no mourner for a friend?

The sanctitude, the multitude
The flattery, the battery
The dream weaver, the under-achiever
The healer, the killer

The well, the sick
The bang, the click
Is there not two inside us all
Only to beckon if we call?

We need only to learn
And not fear to speak
Because for what we yearn
Often differs from what we seek

# Facet 4: The Pit of Despair

The darkest times in my life began when I first met my son's father in 1997. From then on, I proceeded to get myself out of one toxic relationship just to fall into another one (getting married to my oldest daughter's father in 1999 followed by then marrying my third husband in 2001). Though I have had three prior marriages before my current one, the 2$^{nd}$ marriage thankfully was not toxic, but was definitely a mistake. At least I did not walk away from that relationship with any physical or emotional scars, like I did with the others. "You Can't Hurt Me Anymore" is my tale of survival against not one, or two, but THREE awful monsters masquerading as men. My continued hurt was also captured in the poems "Ramblings of a Broken Heart" and "A Stranger." Being that all three of those asshats were basically equally awful, you could apply the feelings contained in "A Stranger" and attribute my words to the experience I had with any one of or all of them. It also reveals how awful one can feel when they realize they have changed everything about themselves to be what they think someone else wants so many times that they do not even recognize themselves or know who they are anymore. "Ramblings of a Broken Heart" was written while I was with my third husband and covers my feelings about what life was like during the period of time approximately 1 year before we finally purchased our first house.

The poem "My Guardian" I dedicate to my dad, who in the midst of all of this chaotic toxicity, passed away in 2000, and whose loss I have felt every single day of the 22 years that has passed since he left. I felt his strength and presence many times throughout those two decades…comforting me, helping me to have the courage to endure, and making sure I did not fail and break my promise to God, because the sadness of my situation often drove me back to the thought of suicide. My dad's love, and God's love, was there for me...the only bright light I had in the darkness that I was trapped in. It was that love that ultimately saved me from the pit of despair and brought me into a life that I could only have pictured in my most Hollywood-laced and over-romanticized dreams. I also wrote a tribute poem to him which came to me following a very intense dream in which I was once again transported to that same spot in heaven that I had visited when God spoke to me and saved me from my suicide to give me a second chance. I was once again sitting on that large rock, with that beautiful clearing surrounding me...but this time, it was my dad talking to me and comforting me. With the anniversary of his passing coming nearer that year, this was comfort I desperately needed, and I feel blessed that I was able to put that experience into words – in the poem "My Father's Eyes".

# You Can't Hurt Me Anymore

My son Aaron's father Dan
I met in 1997
I thought he was the man
My match made in heaven

Little did I know, it was not to be
He had a porn addiction
And was extremely cruel to me
Perpetuating constant pain infliction

He lied about where he'd been
When he didn't come home
He mocked me when
I told him I felt alone

Just a child himself, but wanted our son
Yet acted like a crazed ape
Our relationship was nearly done
Just before my nightmare rape

He arranged a friend to come in to do it
All because he owed him fifty bucks he couldn't pay
It was his decision to put me through it
And take my dignity away

If messing with my heart wasn't enough
Next, he targeted my mind
Things began to get really rough
I looked for answers, but none did I find

He told me he was a demon from hell
And would kill me one day
All I could think was that he was not well
And that I had to get away

Surviving long enough to have my boy
And write his name down on the paper
Never thinking his dad would treat me like a sex toy
By forcing himself on me six days later

He ripped open my stitches
I got an infection
But those who tell end up dead in ditches
So I kept silent for my own protection

In an amusing twist...I was supposedly 'too difficult'
So he ended our relationship and left
And there I was, a broken adult
Soul-weary and bereft

Before I could blink, a knock at my door
After only a few months of peace
I was warmed by the smile he wore
And assumed my happiness could only increase

I had known David in high school
We were very close friends
He told me he knew he had been a fool
To never speak of his true intents

He had liked me since we met
In more than a friendship way
He was there to ask me to let
Him have a chance to hear what he had to say

He knew I had my son to care for
And didn't want us to be alone
He wanted to see what life had in store
For the three of us, on our own

Six months later, we were husband and wife
And in less than 90 days
I realized I had ruined my life
In one of the most horrible ways

He was a monster deep down inside
The list of his crimes unending
The first thing I knew I could never abide
Was that he raped the best man from our wedding

He never told me he was bi-sexual
Or that he wanted to be a swinger
He acted like all that was supposed to be natural
To a woman who had been through the ringer

I'd like to say I was smarter this time
And had the courage to walk away
But in my pocket, I had less than a dime
In my future, I had no say

One day in the kitchen, dinner burned
Inside the hot skillet
That was the first day I learned
It was his goal to find innocence and kill it

The hot pan smashed the right side of my face
I almost lost my eye
Laying on the floor in unconscious disgrace
So, I couldn't even ask him why

He thought he ended me
Maybe he was going to brag
He thought I was dead, you see
When he started to put me in a trash bag

He was surprised to see me stir
And made up some excuse
That day passed in a blur
Replaced by even more abuse

I even forgave him for cheating
I tried to love him past that
All I'd get was another beating
And labels like useless and fat

One day things took the darkest turn
As he prepared to do his worst
It was that day that I did learn
A heart can't just break, it can burst

Pushed face down on the carpet
Enduring horrors for what felt like days
To this day I can't shake the shame
I feel from him hurting me so many ways

Mocked when he was done
Forced to clean up the blood
He said he had to run
And shut the door with a thud

The physical damage done that day
Caused me over twenty more years of issues
But if you think that's the saddest thing I have to say
Then you better go grab some tissues

Once again, I got lucky that he chose to leave
Marched the new girl in to help him move
A new face for him to deceive
Somewhere else for him to get his groove

He was ready to leave and drop me like I didn't matter
Not caring I was pregnant with a little girl
Whose life he was also about to shatter
That didn't even stop him from the insults he'd hurl

I got through the next year recklessly
Marriage on the rebound
Thinking of happiness endlessly
Hoping I was safe and sound

After a few months, we knew our mistake
I filed for divorce; he moved out
At that point, I'd had all I could take
And was filled with a bunch of doubt

When would I ever find the one?
Or what if there wasn't someone for me?
I had searched almost everywhere under the sun
For a love that was meant to be

Months of useless one-night stands
My self-esteem in the trash
I started to revive my former plans
While I worked overtime for extra cash

In an online chat room, I met Chris
I thought he was heaven-sent
Settled into what I assumed would be bliss
And prepared to be content

He cheated on me within the first year
Though he refused to acknowledge his wrong
Turns out he was an exhibitionist and a voyeur
And acted like I should have known all along

Tried to make me feel like I over-reacted
To him chatting with girls and jerking off on cam
While I was off working, he slacked
And pulled the wool over my eyes, like a scam

Another porn addiction...but told me he wasn't into it
Looked at it for hours a day, until minutes before I came home
Didn't make me feel loved, just more and more like shit
Because after hours of other women, he wanted to be alone

When I asked if he loved me, he said yes...never no or maybe
So, I thought up the worst solution
And suggested we have a baby
Which turned out to be my marriage's execution

As the years passed by, he got worse
Screaming obscenities at me lost its punch
I knew then this was just another curse
He had settled for me, but didn't even like me much

Narcissists aren't capable of feeling
All they do is manipulate
My broken soul just left reeling
I saw what he was too late

His charisma helped him keep on the mask
He was always popular, liked by his friends
Always eager to do any task
They thought he was nice, like he pretends

Behind closed doors, a demon
He beat me, and the girls
'No' was not an option, he forced in the semen
Impossible to shut out the hate he hurls

The pattern became ignore, demand, ridicule
My expectations were to grovel, serve and accept
Any kindness ever sprinkled on me became miniscule
His bedroom prowess, half-assed and inept

My self-esteem and health, he erased
My dysfunction he did shape
Just when I thought I couldn't be further disgraced
That's when he escalated to rape

2007 brought a bad health diagnosis for me
And a medication I should have never had
In time, we would both see
It quickly turned good me into bad

Behavioral side effects from the meds
Caused me to be nearly manic
Turned me into a girl who beds
Anyone from a chef to a mechanic

My body wanted attention
My heart just wanted to be adored
I sank into a depression
The further into adultery I got, the more I got bored

Fired from my job, a blessing in disguise
Could not afford the pills anymore
After months, I began to realize
How I'd gone from housewife to whore

I wanted to tell him but knew he would beat me
I prayed I could keep him from finding out
But one day, a persistent text he did see
And that erased any doubt

His reaction was what I expected
He was ready to just let loose
It was all about him feeling rejected
Which in his mind justified abuse

This time, he got arrested
And after the first year passed, he blamed me for it all
I was now even more detested
I had never felt so small

I prayed and prayed for an exit
I begged for true love to find me
After seventeen years of hell, he was ready to quit
Because he reconnected with his first love, Bethany

Now I was expendable, he didn't need me anymore
He proceeded to break up a second couple
Just so he could finally score
Not caring about causing all the trouble

And so came not one but two divorce cases
Which finally ended decades of my lack of waiting
If you want to know the next step of this tale
Then read my poem "Ode to Online Dating"

Now to deliver this phrase
To Dan, David, and Chris
You'll be afraid for the rest of your days
Because God knows every wrong you've done, and his justice doesn't miss!

I won't waste one more moment on any of you
I've cleared out the emotional baggage, there's the door
And now the world even knows it too
You can't hurt me anymore!

# Ramblings of a Broken Heart

I can't look back and remember when it happened
Or pinpoint the moment things changed
When things in my life grew saddened
And everything got re-arranged

I can't point the finger of blame
It used to be so clear
Now there's no one to name
Only me standing here

In every moment of sadness and pain
The only person there each time was me
And it's starting to drive me insane
Because it's something I could never see

No matter how much love I give
I seem to bring out the worst in him
Why do I love him more each day I live
When his love for me is growing dim?

I live on memories of times that made me smile
When I was the most important thing in his heart
How far those memories go back- it's been a while
And feeling like I am losing him tears me apart

I feel like I can't do anything right
My thoughts, words and deeds- all wrong
Whether it be turning out the light
Or trying to sing a song

Things never used to be this complicated
The words never hurt this much

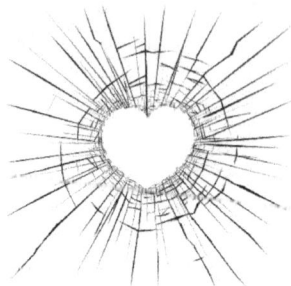

Love used to leave me elated
Just thinking of his touch

My passion for him has not cooled
But my heart is aching
Sometimes I wonder if I've been fooled
By someone out to do all the taking

My emotions left bare
My tears rolling down so fast
I am broken at his feet, and he doesn't care
He doesn't want this to last

All I can feel though is love
And I refuse to give up while it's in me
It's a special gift from above
And I keep praying he will see

He can wait to be happy
Until the new house comes
And keep feeling crappy
And acting dumb

But if that never comes to be
And this is all we get
Can't we just be thankful for "you and me"
So we don't end this life with regret?

I don't mean to make him angry
But I don't deserve his pain
I don't want him to keep on hating me
Because it will drive me insane

I pray each day that he will realize
How much I truly care
And that the next time I look in his eyes
His love I will see there

Before I lay down to sleep tonight
I will pray again
That we can start treating each other right
And that now is the time we'll begin

# A Stranger

When our days were new
And everything seemed right
All I knew was loving you
And being held in your arms so tight

Now those hands that loved me
Have caused me to bleed and bruise
I keep waiting for you to stop and see
Just what you have to lose

Any time we fight now
I can smell the danger
I just can't figure out how
In my life you've become a stranger

The voice that once echoed with love
Shouts bad words and names
I've asked help from the heavens above
To calm the temper I know I can't tame

The eyes that looked at me in wonder
Like I was something brand new
Haven't lowered in months to ponder
Why I am now stiffly under your shoe

The caress I miss so much
Has turned into a fist
How I miss your once soft touch
And the comfort of your kiss

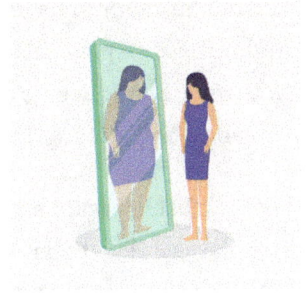

The strength I used to feel inside
Has begun to wither away
I used to hold my head up with pride
Now I rarely look up day to day

The old 'me' would have stood against this
And refused to play this game
Now my ridicule seems endless
Forced to bow down in shame

Looking back, I realize
The blame doesn't all rest with you
When the mirror reflection meets my eyes
I see there's a stranger there, too

# My Guardian

Emptiness since you left here

My damp face still holds a tear

The pain is still fresh, though it's been three years

Never knew how much I'd miss you

Now that you aren't here for me to kiss you

I can't tell you funny stories

Or hear tales of your former glories

You aren't here to watch your grandkids grow

Or even just to let them know

That you see them when they play

And that your love shines on them day by day

But I still feel you at my side

As a driving force in my life

And I know you are one of God's angels up above

At times, I still feel your presence of love

You may be gone from here and not to return again

But one thing is for sure – You are still my guardian

Your love knows no distance

Your help knows no limit

Still always willing to take a chance

To help uplift my spirit

I thank you for remembering me as I remember you

You show heaven, the world and all that inhabit it

That a family's love stays true

# My Father's Eyes

When I came into the world
He was there to hold me
He always wanted a little girl
Or at least that's what my parents told
me

The times when Mom wouldn't listen
Or even try to understand
Instead of giving me a whippin'
Dad was there to lend a hand

I remember the day I left home
And the shame I couldn't disguise
Was reflected ten times worse than anything I'd known
In my father's eyes

I remember the day that mom told dad
That my son and I were alone
I had lost the love I thought I'd had
But dad said I could always come home

I remember the day that mom told him
That my husband had left me with child
Mom thought I lived life on a whim
Or that I was just running wild

Dad tried to hold in his anger
Toward his former son-in-law
Inside thinking sooner than later
He'd be clocking that fool in the jaw

I remember the day he found out I was engaged
At 2 months pregnant, no less
I thought my parents would be enraged
But my dad wished me every success

I remember the day I got the call
That's changed my life to this day
The words pretty much said it all
"Your father has passed away"

Then going to the viewing
To measure dad for a shirt,
I knew it would be my undoing
If mom saw how much I was hurt

When we went on the day of the service
I could see a scar through his hair part
I hurried to fix it, so nervous
that if Mom saw, it would re-break her heart

We put rose petals across his chest
And roses in his hands
Preparing him for eternal rest
Free from time's falling sands

I tried not to cry as I put in his lapel
A baby blue carnation
I knew that he would no longer be able to tell
It looked the same as the one he wore at his wedding celebration

We all sang a song to honor his life
And then paused to wipe away our tears
Gave a moment of silence to remember the strife
He had fought through all these years

But when it came time to give the speech
I didn't know if I could remember
After all what words of mine could reach
Into the gates of heaven?

I honored him for his wisdom and courage
I acknowledged he had no more pain
Silent in the knowledge
That missing him was driving me insane

Just before they closed the lid
And fired blank rifle shots into the skies
A quiet farewell I bid
Knowing I would never again see my father's eyes

When my daughter was born
I took her to his resting place
Knowing that he saw every tear shorn
That was falling down my face

I wanted him to see her
As silly as that may sound
Because she is my world
Now that he is no longer around

Every visit I've made since then
I've tried to make a release
How are you supposed to get closure when
The person you owe your life to is deceased?

I dreamt one night I was crying
Sitting on a rock alone
When I heard a voice behind me saying
"Why are you here on this stone?"

I couldn't look up to answer
I only muttered that I had let someone down
I couldn't face this stranger
And really didn't want him around


When I heard the stranger's voice again
I couldn't believe the reply
He said "May you have peace within
and see yourself through My Father's Eyes"

I looked up to recognize my dad
As he had never been
He no longer looked sick, worn out, or sad
And had a look of wisdom from within

I felt honored to be near him
Even more than I had in life
He promised me sink or swim
He would help me through my strife

"Even though you cannot see me
I will be with you 'til the end
Then we will both be free
And in heaven together again"

When I woke up, I was crying
But had a peace I couldn't disguise
That only grew stronger in spying
A picture of my dad; and there were tears in my father's eyes

# Facet 5: Sweet Escapes

Everyone has their escapes from reality, depression or pain. For me, my escapes have always been either music, dance or writing. I use them as a means of expressing the deep feelings which are always lurking in me just beneath the surface. Although I have danced since I was 7 years old, working my way up to the semi-professional level, I really connect most to music and writing. I have written some songs, but they don't quite pack the emotional "punch" that poetry does and are not quite as therapeutic. I love listening to songs by artists that really seem to capture the particular mood or moment I am in, I find it very comforting. I do play guitar (not well), keyboard (a bit better) and drums (very well), but my greatest musical connection at the moment is singing. I was blessed with a very unique vocal gift at age sixteen (tone mimicry) and I really love being able to harmonize and sound like some of my favorite singers. "Zoning Out" is about my connection to music and how it helps me sometimes to work my way through tough feelings. The other thing I would do would be to daydream… to hope and pray that my life was not just resigned to being some douchebag's punching bag and doormat and that maybe one day, I would actually find the love of my life (or he would find me) and we would finally get to have a loving, normal marriage and life together. That is the background behind the poem "The Meaning of Life". "Daydreamer" covers my obsession with the Caribbean and making it to St. Lucia someday. I have always been drawn to the beach and thinking about it really relaxes me. I celebrate my son and my youngest daughter in the poems "The Man He Will Never Be" and "You Shine". I want the world to know these two amazing, wonderful souls as I have been blessed to

know them all their lives. They both survived the darkest and worst situations that no kids should have to endure and came out of it beside me...all three of us diamonds in the rough.

# Zoning Out

Broken and weary
Sitting under a cloudy sky
Need to see much more clearly
As I let time pass by

I turn on the music
So the pain can drain away
I shut out the rhetoric
For yet another day

The vocals are my diary
Laying bare my weary soul
As the song plays, I can see
I'm beginning to regain control

The guitar strums are hate
The saxophone blares fear
The drums beat out my fate
The keyboard draws me near

All at once, my sadness leaves
Music has drawn a path across my vein
I choke back sobs and heaves
As the memories remain

The music confessed my pain
With lyrics that cut deep inside
As the tears pour down like rain
The future is mine to decide

# The Meaning of Life

Taking a walk on the soft warm sand
Living each second to hold your hand
Revealing my secrets to a soul I can trust
Knowing that the only thing that matters is "us"

Picturing each day and night together
Days of laughter, nights of pleasure
What could be more perfect than this
Savoring the passion of every kiss

I picture our lives, joined as one
Enjoying the rising and setting of the sun
Staying up late to watch the stars
And thanking God that we are where we are

Seeing our family in my mind's eye
Knowing a joy that will make me cry
Loving you forever with everything in me
Showing you the side of me no one else will ever see

Being content in knowing that everything I do
Exists for the sake of loving you
Investing in the greatest dream you've made come true
Together forever, doing everything we wanted to

If you want the meaning of life
Then I will tell you true
I plan to become your wife

And spend eternity loving you

You're the reason that I'm alive
The reason I am here
You're the reason why
I have no more fear

You're my reason for breathing
You're what makes life worth living
You give my purpose meaning
You're worth the effort I'm giving

One day soon, you'll hold my hand
And I will take your name
Together forever we will stand
Never again to be the same

How lucky I am to have you
How blessed I'll be to keep you
And I'll spend my life showing you
Anything worth doing is for the love of you

I will love you without condition
I will hold you without expectation
I will keep you throughout eternity
Just content to know your loving me

No one will ever love you more
Or see the depth in your beautiful eyes
We are soul mates, for sure
And it took God to recognize

My love for you knows no limit
My devotion knows no end
You are my heart and spirit
And always my best friend

We'll be together past the end of time
Our love will outlast all things
Together in perfection, sublime
Fate giving our love its wings

# *Daydreamer*

Daydreamer Pisces
What adventures will you conjure today?
As you wish to be in places
Tropical and far away

You've thought of so many
All throughout the years
The world is full of islands plenty
Beachy places to cry your tears

St. Lucia has always been the dream
Chasing the waterfalls
Watching the sunlight beam
Over places big and small

Playing in the ocean
Laying in the sun
Thankful life has slowed its motion
Living life for fun

Anywhere in the Caribbean
We're gonna get there someday
Before our stress sinks us into oblivion
It's time our inner child got to play

# The Man He Will Never Be

My firstborn, my son
There is so much I want to say
I want you to know you're the one
That helped to make me who I am today

I was just a stupid kid
Wild and immature
Further into the darkness I slid
But your birth was the cure

I knew you were going to need me
So, I tried to figure life out fast
I tried to become who I needed to be
To finally outrun my past

I didn't get to be the mother I wanted to be
There are so many times I failed
Try as I might, I just couldn't see
How to fix where my life had derailed

In spite of not being there when I should have been
You have become a man I truly admire
Each losing situation, you turned into a win
And your success spread like wildfire

I know it's been such a shitshow
But I'm proud of who I see
Looking back, it's ironic now that I know
I needed you more than you needed me

You taught me how to be strong
And you never turned your back on me
Just as I suspected all along
You've become the man your dad could never be

# You Shine

As long as there is breath in me
And I have something to share
Just know that I plan to be
Right by your side, always there

I see so much of myself in you
Each and every day I pray
That clouds of grey become skies of blue
For my beautiful Kaylee Renee

I know that you're going to stun the world
You're going to rattle some cages
You are destined for greatness, girl
And you'll get there, in stages

You're special and unique
I hope that you'll always know why
Fashion sense better than a boutique
And not just because you're bi

You have the same issue I did
All those many years ago
When I tried to give up, but God forbid
Me to chicken out and let go

You don't see your beauty
You can't see your worth
Even if your never in a movie
You've been destined for fame since birth

You're going to do something amazing
Success is going to come fast
I can just see you, trail blazing
As you set fire to the pain of your past

No one who hurt you will do so again
They can't touch or even see the real you
I think back on all those many nights when
You survived the worst of what he could do

Why didn't I believe you?
You had the truth down to the letter
You told me if I left, we'd get through
And that I could definitely do better

That is the kind of faith I have in you
Your pain holds you prisoner in your past
But I know you're going to get through
Your life will have an all-star cast

Never give someone the power
To take advantage of you
Surround yourself every day and hour
With those who value what you've been through

Remember that you're the writer
This story is yours to tell
I celebrate you, the fighter
Who stood beside me at the gates of hell

We got through it, stronger
We made it, together
But that's not our lives any longer
We don't ruminate in stormy weather

I believe in what you can do
I'll be cheering you on, Kaylee
I'm pretty sure you know it's true
You can be the woman you're meant to be

Your path is clear
Have faith that you'll be fine
As all those clouds of doubt disappear
So your eyes can see that you shine

# Facet 6: A Love Story

Following my divorce in 2019, which finally freed me from a 17-year toxic marriage which was plagued with domestic violence. I proceeded to move on with my life. I did this in the worst way possible – looking for someone else to solve my problems for me instead of healing myself so that maybe I could have a chance at a normal life. But, as fate would have it, God actually had a surprise in store for me. The one. No, not Neo...though I can't say I would be sad to get Keanu Reeves, I wanted someone just as sexy but way more low-key. My ONE and only. The one that I dreamt of all those days I was being taken for granted, disrespected, and tormented and all those nights I spent wishing that I was laying next to literally anyone else but who I was stuck next to. My soulmate made his appearance in my life. Coincidentally, we met on a day where two very significant things in my life occurred. First, it was the day my college lists as the day I officially graduated with my bachelor's degree. Second, it was the day that the guy who I had been dating for about 4 months decided to break up with me with absolutely no warning and in the most heartless way possible. Interestingly enough, his ex-reached out to me to tell me what horrible things he had been saying to her about me, which is when we put two and two together and realized that the equation equaled him being a rat, a dog and a liar. He had been dating BOTH of us at the same time...telling me that they were not together but he could not post pictures of us on his Facebook because she was psycho and possessive and did not get that they were over while telling her that I was just some barfly he met one night that decided to catch feelings for him off a one night stand, and that he tried to dodge me, ditch me, break up with me but I was not getting the message.

After getting down to the truth of things, I realized I was not going to shed one single tear over a liar. So, I turned all my dating profiles back on THAT DAY and said to myself, 'the hell with it! There has to be someone out there for me!' My wonderful husband sent me a message that day, through Facebook Dating. We talked almost a continuous 48 hours straight (except a few hours sleeping time for us both and a little work for me the second day). We talked a little on the phone the 2nd day, and I told him I wanted to go on a date...meet face to face. Since he had moved here from the east coast and didn't have a car, I drove to where he was staying to pick him up. The moment this man got into the car, smiled at me and took my hand, I knew right then and there that he was exactly who I had spent my whole life searching for. He kissed me and I literally forgot all words to the English language, my name, and what planet I was on for about a full sixty seconds. The drive back to my house you would think would be nerve-wracking or awkward...but it was anything but. It was like it had always been that way, but at the same time the feeling of 'so that is what has been missing.' We watched movies and ate. He stayed the night. And the next night, and two more nights. By October 31st, 6 days after meeting online and 4 days after meeting in person, we were driving back to where he had been renting a room to pick up all his stuff. He moved in with me and neither of us looked back, just forward. On our wedding day, we were able to honestly say that our first date was still in progress since he had never left my side. Not many people can say that and not many have a love story as charming as ours. "Ode to Online Dating" is the story of the last year of searching for 'Mr. Right' before he finally arrived. The other poems in this section were written either after he and I found one another or even more interestingly...long before we ever did, at times when I think my soul was dreaming and catching glimpses of what I eventually would have. I had a love story to tell, and the words just poured right out of my heart, which was overflowing with love.

# Ode to Online Dating

Plenty of Fish, you are the stuff of nightmares

First, you brought me a man-child

A forty-five-year-old momma's boy, completely unaware

On a scale of one to spicy, he wasn't even mild

Facebook Dating, then you brought the ex-cop

Who had seven children and no self-control

Who gaslighted me from day one and wouldn't stop

It felt like he was killing my soul

Back to Plenty of Fish, thought I'd try once more

You brought me a hottie then

But this wasn't the boy next door

He was a drunk and a cheater…I almost wanted to swear off men

Ah Facebook Dating…one more try

But wait! What's this? He's…different

Did you ACTUALLY find me THE GUY?!

After all the days, weeks, months and hours spent

His name was Michael

His face, angelic

His charisma known to beguile

His smile a holy relic

We both knew we were in love day one

And oh, how the anticipation grew

I dreamt of everything under the sun

And we hadn't even passed day two

By the time we met face to face
We both knew this is it
This is really going someplace
One hundred and fifty percent legit

That first kiss took me to another dimension
I'm not sure I ever came back
Not the slightest hint of tension
Life was finally on the right track

Fast forward to the first time we made love
I almost passed out when I saw his bod
Sculpted abs from the angels above
He looked better than a fucking Greek God!

I thought to myself...how did I luck out like this?
What does he see in me?
But the look on his face as he would reminisce
On the things of mine he gets to see

A lifetime apart, but now finally together
Walked right into my life, didn't miss a beat
The sun broke through the stormy weather
And now finally, both our lives are complete

Our wedding day, we both shone with glee
Not anticipating much could change
My love for him, his love for me
No surprises at this stage

But no, the moment the minister started
Both of us knew it was the last puzzle piece
Official in the eyes of God and never to be parted
With a love that will never cease

# *Without You*

My life started with fear
And transitioned to pain
Nothing was ever clear
As I slowly went insane

The darkness was all around me
Like a suffocating blanket
I thought that was all I would ever be
Never thought I would make it

You found me
Saved me from the nightmare
Helped breathe life into me
And made me aware

No rhythm
No rhyme
No reason
No logic
No happiness
No kindness
No breathing
No way to make it
Without you

Words cannot express my love
Trying makes me feel so lost
I know this came straight from above
And I will protect it always, whatever the cost

# My Heart

It's 3 AM- counting sheep
wish I could just get some fucking sleep
the dream was too real, now I'm a mess
and how the hell did I get undressed??

Feelings and visions are powerful things
sometimes just a phrase can make your heart grow wings
soaring through the heavens above
reeling through the clouds on rays of love

It feels like forever I've needed you
now it feels like forever I've known you
how many years I spent pleading to
just be sat down and shown you

Making up for time lost is a waste
I want to live for what we have now
And not spend every moment in haste
But not take things TOO SLOW

Passion is an awkward master
It tells each part, each thought- FASTER, FASTER!
I will remember that while holding my pillow tight
And picturing laying in your arms tonight

I do not regret that I told you how I feel
Maybe you question if it is real
I don't blame you for being cautious
But being the first with the courage makes you nauseous

I sit and wonder what's on your mind
Pray that I won't get left behind
I dream of what I want to do to you
And things I hope and wish you'd do too

I want to love you completely
I want to pleasure you sweetly
I want you to orgasm until you almost go insane
So you have no choice but to scream out my name

Pleasure for hours and days
So many positions and ways
Calling out for you in ecstasy
Because you are all I need

You are the best part of me
You are the very heart of me
My soul, my rhyme and reason
Today, next month, next season

Taking a walk on the soft warm sand
Living each second to hold your hand
Revealing my secrets to a soul I can trust
Knowing that the only thing that matters is "us"

Picturing each day and night together
Days of laughter, nights of pleasure
What could be more perfect than this
Savoring the passion of every kiss

How lucky I am to have you
How blessed I'll be to keep you
And I'll spend my life showing you
Anything worth doing is for the love of you

I will love you without condition
I will hold you without expectation
I will keep you throughout eternity
Just content to know your loving me

My love for you knows no limit
My devotion knows no end
You are my heart and spirit
And always my best friend

We'll be together past the end of time
Our love will outlast all things
Together in perfection, sublime
Fate giving our love its wings

# *Last*

Holding your hand
Kissing your face
Making a plan
For a new place
Sorry you were not the first
But you will be the last

Making love to you
Knowing that you love me
Feeling something so true
Knowing that it is meant to be
Sorry you are not the first
But you will be the last

Making a dream real
Living each day happy
I cannot help how strongly I feel
Though I know it may seem sappy
And you may not be the first
But you will be the last

I see us together on the beach
Watching a perfect sunset
You never out of my arms' reach
Dreaming of what we haven't done yet
This is a first
And will not be a last

Becoming a family together

Happy and in love
Knowing that forever
We need to thank the Lord above
This for both of us is a first
And will also be a last

Waking up each day to your smile
Enjoying a morning kiss
Even when you're only gone a while
You know that it's you that I miss
Our relationship is a special first
And I know in my heart it will always last

# Believing

I didn't believe in happy endings
Languishing over past loves and dreams
And regretted most of the time I'd been spending
Just wishing for the simple things

A nice house with a great lawn
A switch to turn my sprinklers on
Surprising someone with breakfast in bed
Deciding you'd rather stay there instead

A fireplace lit on a cold winter night
My beloved's face in candlelight
Champagne glasses filled to the top
The start of a passion that doesn't stop

These are things I tried to forget
That I had accepted I would never get
Suddenly up and out of the blue
Reality changed when I met you

I began to believe that dreams could become real
That someone else out there does feel what I feel
I dared to think the future may not be tragic
Knowing I could be the one to make the magic

Picturing a soft caress
Moments lost in tenderness
Breathless, intense, I cry out in the rain
But this time in pleasure, no longer in pain

Waking up to a perfect sunrise
Seeing everything that's real and true in your eyes
Falling asleep to a perfect sunset
To dream of the things we haven't done yet

Never thought it could be real
Never thought this could be true
Until I saw the way you could make me feel
When you made me believe in you

# What You Are to Me

Your eyes are like the stars to me

They shine as if they call to me

Your smile is the warmth of a thousand lost summers
I never experienced

It warms me with a joyous admiration I can only pray
not to lose

Your voice is the slow reassurance that lovingly puts me to sleep at night

And gently calls me to consciousness in the morning

Your touch is my security blanket

The protection I've sought since birth

Your words touch me in places people can't

With a deep and everlasting impression that leaves me wanting more

Your thoughts are a mystery to me

I pointlessly sit and ponder if I am in them

Your dreams are a challenge to us both –

You dare to dream them, and I strive for your happiness to make them real

Your future is an open book to you, with its pages blank

But to me it's a prayer – that in time, I may write my place there

Your kiss is life to me

Recharging my ever-weary soul to keep going on

Yourself – you are everything to me

Life, love and happiness flowing through me…

…this is what you are to me.

# Facet 7: Waking Nightmares

Even the best fairy tale is going to have its bumps in the road. The twists and turns that make you jump and gasp and wonder if the couple will ever get their happily ever after. Well, in the case of my husband and I, our bump in the road came in September of 2022. My husband Michael has Type 1 bipolar disorder, which he was diagnosed with in September of 2007. He had not been on any medication for it since the first manic episode he had then. The fallout from that first episode caused him to disappear from his entire family for 15 years and move 300 miles away to try to start over again. Since it was so long ago, and he had not had an episode since the first one, I was naive and stupid enough to think that he was now fine, and that nothing like that could ever happen again. As the stress he was under began to make him buckle and falter, he brought up more and more that he was concerned another episode may be on the horizon, but I just ignored this, not even truly understanding what an episode was...what would happen to someone during this time? What would it be like for him, for me, for Kaylee? Sadly, we got the answer to that question...and if not for the strength of our love and the grace of God, we likely would not have come out on the other side of this still together. Thankfully, we did.

I believe what has drawn me even closer to my husband since this episode happened was being able to see the deep loathing and pain within him that so closely mirrored my own and everything that I have tried to keep buried inside me so no one would see. Knowing that another person, especially one that I adore with all my heart, could feel something so profound and feel it even deeper and darker than I feel my own caused my heart to just go out to him with so much sadness and regret that no matter how much love I showered him with or how badly I prayed that something I could do could help to take the sadness and pain away from him, the episode had its own time table for when it would finally lift its cursed storm cloud and let us be. All he and I could do was batten down the hatches and hunker down until the storm passed.

The poems in this section were written during the manic episode and captured my feelings during that time and a lot of the warped things that can come out of the mind of someone who is in the throes of this disorder. If you are not familiar with bipolar disorder, please do not make the mistake I did and think it just means someone may be "a little moody" from time to time. Think worst case scenario. Think of the exact OPPOSITE of how they normally think, act, communicate, treat people, see the world and their place in it. If you have a diamond in the rough...a true prince charming...when he goes manic, he will not know or care who you are, who he is, what is real or consequences of the actions of anything he does. After braving that, and the deepest, darkest depression you could ever fathom, then they are left feeling drained. Often, they don't remember large parts of what happened either...so they have no idea what they have put you through while they were in their own hell. So, you will see the impact this had on me in the poems "Prisoner" and "Purgatory". "Soul Cleaver", is more of a story poem. It is like a 'squaring off' between he and I when he was at some of his worst moments during the episode, and my determination that he would not be forever lost to this disorder and my resolve that the darkness would not take him away from me. When the bipolar episode ended and we both started to heal from the fallout, "In My Heart" speaks of that time and my feelings as we both started picking up the pieces and re-building our marriage.

In the year prior to and especially in the 8 months before the manic episode kicked off, Michael and I were having to deal with the heavy burden of the non-stop antics and machinations of my oldest daughter. Though I struggled her entire life to help her rise above the dark half of her genetics, protect her from that hateful influence and save her from herself...in the end she was determined to throw me away, crucify me for her failures and loneliness, then try to turn my youngest daughter Kaylee into a carbon-copy of her. All of that bowel-twisting, gut-wrenching, stomach-turning bullshit finally came to an end the day before Samantha had a daughter of her own. It is sad knowing I am a grandmother in fact, but not in reality...as she and her toxic boyfriend have decided that they never want me to see their baby. Cutting one of your own flesh and blood kids out of your life is definitely not something any parent wants to do, but when someone has kicked you in the face, ripped out your heart for the 100th time with zero remorse and happily decided that they want to jump into the quicksand and mire themselves...sometimes you have to just walk away and let them sink.

"Wolf in Sheep's Clothing" is the story of how my oldest daughter became estranged to me after everything she put herself, me, my husband and my youngest daughter through. She chose toxicity over stability and fake friends over family, and she is going to have to live with that choice for the rest of her life. I do not wish her ill, even to this day. All I wanted for all of us was peace, but unfortunately, it was not possible for her and peace to exist in the same space due to the choices she continued to make. The final straw which told me there was never going to be a chance for a 'prodigal son' moment with her was when she did not invite me to her baby shower, banned me from her baby's life because her boyfriend hates me and because I stood against her and protected my youngest daughter from her toxicity, THEN decided to reach out to her biological father, the man who physically destroyed me and abused me in every conceivable fashion. The man who did not want to ever visit her when she was younger. This is who she claims as 'family", forgetting all the sacrifices I made throughout her life to protect her from him so that she could have a chance at a normal childhood. Unfortunately, that failed for two reasons... her choices and rebellion against anything good I tried to teach her, and the toxicity of my marriage to my third husband. The latter is NOT an excuse for her choosing to be the person she is, but I know it did have a hand in warping an already twisted mind.

# Wolf in Sheep's Clothing

Things started off like they normally do

Tiny, smiling baby and an exhausted, smiling mother

But it turns out the pain you would put me through

Cut me deeper than any other

You don't expect that a part of you can betray

Your own DNA turned against you

You threw my love away

Like blowing your nose on a tissue

I used to think I lost your love

And I cried each time you'd fall

But I can say as true as the heavens above

That you never even loved me at all

I say that because you're not capable of it

Some seeds they just say are bad

Which is why I had to quit

Once I knew you were exactly like your dad

The fact that you could turn to him and his ilk

After the horrible things they've done

Then stooping so low as to con and bilk

Some money out of my daughter and son

You swore it was for your baby fund

But there is not a time in your life you could hold on to money

Anything good, wholesome or righteous you shunned

Running around with a group of idiots, thinking everything is funny

Finding out you were pregnant was no wake up call
You said "having a baby will be fun"
I can't believe you had the gall
To inflict the two of you as parents on an innocent one

I guess I should have expected it
You faked goodness and serenity
I didn't learn you were full of shit
Until I found out you'd thrown away your virginity

Chasing a guy who didn't care about you
He'd get close then stick you back on the shelf
There wasn't anything you weren't willing to do
Until the day the drug drama disgraced his family, and he killed himself

You've spent your whole life as a liar
And I don't expect that will ever change
I had to set the bad memories of you on fire
And decide to just estrange

You pushed me to my limit
You never cared for your sister
Even when your style she tried to mimic
All you and your crew did was diss her

Got her high, breaking into cars
Took her on a beer run
Underage drinking, inflicting emotional scars
Just more ways for you to get your fun

It wasn't enough one of your scumbag friends
Ended up hurting poor Kaylee
You turned blame for it on HER to further your own ends
And still hang with the guy, even though he's beyond shady

You urged her to get away from me
Told her to hurry, before it was too late

And if you couldn't break her free
Then she should try to emancipate

You worsened her depression
She was months behind in school
Then imitating your best impression
She began to be cold and cruel

She snuck out and lied to us
She constantly disobeyed
She yelled and argued and cussed
She couldn't see she was being played

Until you and those misfits sunk so low
When sneaking her out of the house
You sent that piece of shit molester to her window
And made her hang out with the louse!

She wanted your friendship and approval so bad
She was willing to try to accept his 'I'm sorry'
But every time she'd go hang out, all she had
Was more people causing her anxiety and worry

She was ignored for basketball
Or left near the asshole, to suffer his stare
She knew you didn't care at all
She couldn't feel safe there anywhere

Why the hell was she risking punishment
To get a few hours with you
When what she got was homophobic judgement
And more hoops to jump through

She wanted your approval
She looked up to you, until she could see
The only choice we could make was your removal
From her life so she could become what you wouldn't ever be

She still has a chance
She still has a prayer
You threw away your life to a romance
With an unambitious player

I asked myself if I could see any real good in you
But sadly, the answer was no
I prayed it was something you'd work through
But instead, you became my mom 2.0

I wished so much better for you
I tried to help you achieve it
But if there was someone willing to be a fool
You'd lie straight to their face, and they believed it

You couldn't ever be honest
Even when confronted with the lie
After years of disrespect, I noticed
And prepared to say goodbye

To avoid it, I gave chance after chance
And prayed you would come around
But after years of this dance
I could tell you'd rather stay lost than be found

You're just a wolf in sheep's clothing
Running wild with your idiot pack
So naive, never seeing or knowing
I made excuses for you and cut you so much slack

Those days are at an end
I've stopped trying, but wished you luck
One day, you'll end up with no one, not a single friend
And you'll be looking for me to give a fuck

But all I can wish for you today
Is that you got your happily ever after

Though you tried to ruin mine, your jealousy can't stand in my way

So, farewell. I wish you the best, Samantha.

# Prisoner

Banging on the glass

Let me out

Shouting that I cannot last

It's not doubt

I have no control

I've been given no choice

I can say this whole thing is getting old

Since I spent most of my life with no
voice

It's not a question of love

That is solid as a rock

Still asking God in heaven above

To help me through this shock

I just want to feel loved again

Heard and understood

So I'll just sit here until then

Waiting for things to go back to good

# Purgatory

Inner voice of doubts

Never whispers, only shouts

You try to drown it out but still it will remain

Knowing the longer I hear it, I am going insane

There are no words which comfort me

Why do I feel so incomplete?

Stupid, fat and lazy

Purpose always hazy

Everything confuses me

Peace eludes me

Keep trying but I just can't hide it

I'm the worst kind of mess and I can't fight it

I look in the mirror and hate what I see

Keep wanting to change but in the end, it's always me

Everyone is sick of hearing my voice

Everyone is pretending that I have a choice

"Just shut up and stop feeling like that"

"Calm down, I only said you're a little fat"

"Shut up and stop sneezing!"

"While you're at it, hold your breath and stop breathing"

"I don't need to hear it when I've heard it before"

"Why do you have to be a psychotic bore?"

"You have trust issues, but yet I chose to lie"

"Let me take what's unbearable and make it amplified"

"I don't understand why you're a mess today"

"Oh, you're in darkness? Let me gaslight your way"

"Ask any more questions, and I'll see that you burn"

"I don't give a fuck if that's how you learn"

"Since I think I know your feelings, the rest doesn't matter"

"Since I've reassured you already, you just need to move faster"

"Why do you waste my time?"

"Just smile and act like you're fine"

"Turn off the sadness, ignore the pain"

"Watch my lack of empathy drive you insane"

"Stop crying, pull yourself together"

"Or I'm going to leave you standing in stormy weather"

"I don't care about your doubts"

"Shut the fuck up, I'm walking out"

"Hurry and change your attitude in a flash"

"And if you don't like it, you can kiss my ass"


Yes...I know that this is all for God's glory

But I'm just the last soul trapped in this purgatory

# *Soul Cleaver*

He arrived on a pure white steed
Sword held aloft in the air
He said he knew all I would need
And that he would always be there

Whirlwind romance followed by
months of bliss
Dream wedding and an enviable life
Feeling cherished with each and every
kiss
Knowing that I am blessed to be his
wife

I'm not sure exactly what changed
But it happened in the blink of an eye
We went from happily in love to
estranged
And there is no one that can explain why

I understand that life's stress was too much
He took on more than any one person should take
Instead of feeling his warm and loving touch
His words kept hammering to make me break

You can't hold a grudge when it's driven by illness
Try to tell yourself not to take it to heart, but you do
The once beautiful dream now sits a fucking mess
Why does he mock all I've been put through?

He swore no one would ever hurt me again

And that he'd love me beyond all time
It's impossible to feel safe when
All reason has lost its rhyme

When will the madness end
And love return to his heart?
He's my soulmate and my best friend
But he's tearing me apart

I can see the real him is still in there
Looking so trapped and lost behind those eyes
I'm not exactly sure how much he is aware
Or when he will wake up and realize

Will the truth be too much when he is better?
It's not even like I want an apology
Our love is stronger than stormy weather
And I hope that is something he comes to see

Praying for medication that can stabilize
And throw cold reason on his fire of rage
Remove the pain and hate from his eyes
And free him from his bipolar cage

I know he can beat this if he chooses to
Once he sees his family is all he'll ever need
We'll be able to see him through
As long as he stays away from the weed

The thing he thought was helping him
Has left his mind in a dark place
He's changed his whole personality on a whim
And thrown pain on us that I hope time will erase

Our family bond was stronger than most
Our love was the stuff of dreams

I don't want him to remain a ghost
Trapped in his illness, wailing silent screams

He has beaten things tougher than this
And I know if we can help him, he'll be fine
I just hope we can stop this manic episode of his
Before he ends up crossing a tragic line

He says he is the antichrist, what do I do?
Communing with demons in his mind
Blaming us for all he is putting us through
While loudly yelling that "he is fine"

He says not to stand in Hell's way
As 'Satan' takes a selfie
And the only thought in my mind each day
Is DAMN, this is NOT healthy!

"Take me to the mall, so I can hand out these business cards
Even though no one asked me to
Take your broken heart shards
And leave me to what I'm going to do

Let the darkness swallow me
I feel safer there than I do with you
Why is it so hard for you to see
Just what the fuck I am going through?

The neighbors should have told me to stop talking
I don't care if they were afraid of me
All I was out doing was walking
While making sure to stay crazy

It's totally normal to walk up to strangers
And tell them your secrets and life story
They should have ignored the danger

No matter how strange, insane or gory

And I took the oath to Satan
Stop standing up for yourself
My abuse of you is blatant
And if you won't give me what I ask, I'll get it somewhere else

Chivalry is dead because women killed it
Nice guys finish last
Even though I know what I say is a crock of shit
Let me continue to make you ashamed of your past

In my broken mind, you abused me
You took advantage of me and took control
You were too blind to see
How the stress took its toll

Even though I never told you, you should have known
Let me punish you for not reading my mind
Instead of celebrating that our love has grown
It seems easier to leave you behind

I'm giving you another chance to serve
You won't be my queen until you treat me like a king
Yeah, I guess I have a lot of fucking nerve
To act like any of this is a thing

But this is my reality
This is what I choose
You better swear fealty
Or you will surely lose"

Despite what he thinks, this is not where our story ends
Satan has no claim to his soul
He gave it to me when we married, as best friends
And so evil better let him go

I've faced down the Hordes of Hell before
Rebuilt myself from nothing time and again
I have strength too powerful to ignore
And a will too strong to bend

"If the devil wants you
Then he'll have to go through me
He can look into my eyes of blue
And know that only one outcome can be

I will protect you from even yourself
I will catch you when you fall
Set that hate back on the shelf
And realize we truly have it all"

He's up against a formidable foe
But I won't flinch or falter
The devil is gonna let him go
Because he vowed his soul to me on the alter

God will help me save you
He will be our dream weaver
One thing I know is true
You were not meant to be a soul cleaver

You can't destroy our family
You can't destroy our life
I hope by now that you can see
I am more than just your wife

Open up and let go of the darkness
I can help you release the hate
Let's clean up this awful mess
Before it ends up being too late

Who cares about having Facebook friends?
They don't know you like I do
That is not the means to an end
This is not worth what you're putting us through

You've tried to trade being our everything
For being known as a joke and novelty
Look down at your left hand, to your ring
And remember what you promised me

For the longest time now
Your love has seen me through
And from here on, I vow
I'm going to take good care of you

You don't have to keep feeling
All those bad things that you do
Don't let them keep you reeling
Don't let them cleave our souls in two

I'll love you more tomorrow
Than I loved you today
And each time you feel any sorrow
Just know our love will light your way

# In My Heart

These are the words I write
That I wish I could say to you
They come from deep inside
And every last one is true

The love in your eyes warms my heart
And fills my soul with song
We've stood time's test, not to part
And tried to keep our love strong

You love me so much
And I feel so unworthy
You long for my touch
And sometimes I can't breathe

I know you've made mistakes
But I still see you as so pure
You tell me you love me with every breath you take
You're a prince, to be sure

A halo of light from your hair
Your strong arms to hold me
Knowing you'll always be there
You're everything I wish I could be

Your kisses make my heart beat
Until I think it might choke me
And I think it's neat
You even like to sing karaoke!

Still struggling to feel like I belong
With a guy as sweet as you
After all that I did wrong
Why you love me, I haven't a clue

In your eyes, I'm everything
But I will tell you what
I still feel like nothing
Can't run from being a slut

You broke my heart
I kicked yours
You ripped me apart
I did worse

Now you're the only thing holding me together
And I'm trying to come out of my shell
Because I want to stay with you forever
Since you finally woke up and saved us from hell

I will try to be more loving
And tell you the things I don't show
But it's hard when I feel like nothing
To tell you what your heart should know

I know I need to give you more
You deserve more than me
Your love makes my heart soar
Like a prisoner, finally freed

Please be patient with me
I'm harder on me than you
But if you'll stick by me, you'll see
I know I will find the way through

# Facet 8: The Next Chapter

Much as anyone would do after living four decades of nightmares, I catch myself wondering what life holds in store for me now. Thankfully, I no longer fear what might be on the horizon. I know that no matter how many times I thought I couldn't make it through what I was going through, how scared or alone I felt, how many tears I cried or how many years were wasted spinning my wheels...in the end, I made it through. Yes, the scars are deep, and real. It has changed me in ways that I never could have imagined. But something else happened, too. I got to see just how much of a true badass that I am. The fighter in me. The dreamer. The innocent child I thought the world murdered is still within me, ready to live the life that she never got the chance to. I'm surrounded by all the people that love me, and there is nothing left to hold me back or stand in my way. Yes, the future looks bright, and I look forward to the journey there, and all the interesting experiences that I will get to have along the way. I hope you enjoy this last poem, "Future" – and my glimpse into the dreams and wishes I hope may be waiting for me in these next several years and decades of life.

Now that you all know my story, many of you may want to know what happens next, just like I do. Well, stay tuned! Because this is just the first book of many which I will be sending out there into the world to share. I have so many more stories to share...both true and fictional. My one hope is that you were able to take something away from one or more of these poems and that the words contained inside were able to help give you comfort and peace. When I went through my roughest, darkest times...that was the one thing I really needed. To know that I wasn't weak, or defective, or unlovable. But most importantly...to know that I wasn't alone. So rest easy...you are not alone, and as long as we know that, we can get through ANYTHING that life may throw our way. Shine on, everyone. Life is shaping you, but in the end, you'll be the diamond you were born to be...harder than nails and more beautiful than you could ever imagine. Never let someone try to dull your shine. It took so much to get you here...sparkle proudly so the world can see all of those cuts...those facet moments...that made you who you are!

# *Future*

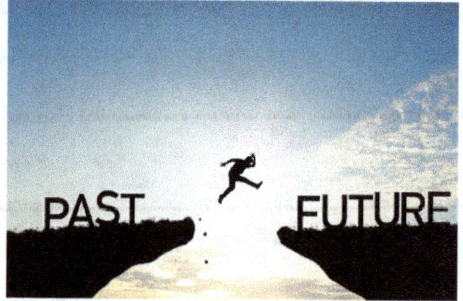

I catch my mind wandering

With my occasional pondering

What's next? What's in store?

Now that I'm off the rough seas and safe on shore

Husband by my side

No more roller coaster ride

Life's surprises only good

Enjoying happiness, like we should

Hammock on St. Lucia

Free from our minutia

Retired and living our dreams

Chasing sun rays and moon beams

Writing yet another book

Weaving words which leave them shook

I hope my stories hit their mark

And shine some light into the deepest dark

Entertain, amuse or frighten

Sometimes surprise, or even enlighten

I've poured it out here, but still have so much to say

Now that I have love to keep lighting my way

Achieving this dream has given me closure

On a lifetime of pain which I'm glad is now over

With the love of my family, I know I'll be fine

My husband and I on date nights, with glasses of wine

My children, out achieving their success

Reaching for greatness and not settling for less

It's been so surreal, watching us mature

Time always passing, bringing us closer to the future

We've ALL come so far

Wished upon a shooting star

Hoped and prayed and sometimes wished

That we would someday achieve something like this

More than success, which is now in reach

We have not just love – but inner peace

We will hold on to this gift, and press on

Life is a battle we've finally won

Now that I've shared these moments, everyone knows

We're not just a family, we're a band of heroes!

# About The Author

## Desiree Batiste

Desiree Batiste was born in Mesa, Arizona in 1979. She currently lives in Buckeye, Arizona with her husband, Michael and her daughter, Kaylee and their three cats: Sketch, Pixel and Trace.

After surviving abuse at the hands of her mother in her teenage years, then surviving three separate relationships plagued with domestic violence, Desiree still persevered and graduated summa cum laude with her Bachelors of Science in Technical Management with Criminal Justice specialization in 2020.

Writing stories and poetry has been a life long passion for Desiree. She had her first poem published in a small circulation newspaper for children at age 9 1/2, which only fueled her interest in writing. She has been diagnosed with PTSD and several anxiety disorders as the result of her past experiences. She continues with therapy on these issues, but writing has always been very therapeutic for her and she hopes by sharing her poems and stories, she will help others who are in similar life circumstances.

Desiree has more books in the making as well. She is working on her autobiography and a psychological thriller fiction novel.

www.ingramcontent.com/pod-product-compliance
Lightning Source LLC
LaVergne TN
LVHW021122080426
835513LV00011B/1197